THE **ROUGH**, THE *SMOOTH* AND THE *QUIRKY*

THE *ROUGH*, THE *SMOOTH* AND THE QUIRKY

Poems for a Complicated World

John Webster

John Webster Publications
Oxford

First published in Great Britain in 2025
by John Webster Publications
© John Webster 2025

The moral right of John Webster
to be identified as the author of this work
has been asserted in accordance with the
Copyright, Designs and Patents Act of 1988.

All rights reserved. No part of this publication
may be reproduced, stored in a retrieval system,
or transmitted in any form or by any means,
electronic, mechanical, photocopying, recording,
or otherwise, without the prior permission of both
the copyright owner and the above publisher
of this book.

ISBN 978-1-0683328-6-9

John Webster Publications
Oxford
Email: webstjohn@gmail.com
Website: www.johnmwebster.co.uk

'In the house of poetry
there are many mansions....'
— H.J.C. Grierson

'Say what you mean
and put a backbeat on it...'
— John Lennon to David Bowie

'Laughter is the best medicine...'
— Lord Byron

INTRODUCTORY

These poems have arisen from difficult, delightful and off-beat events and occurrences, and the 'rough', the 'smooth' and the 'quirky' will be found throughout, sometimes within the same poem. The loss of friends and loved ones was certainly a huge spur to some of them, and the world events that are brought so close to us daily also provoked their responses.

Inspirational figures (and their opposites) also appear, as do stories drawn from history or from travel, which I hope lead in a hopeful direction. Other poems have arisen from some of the most divisive subjects around, (Donald Trump, the trans debate, Wokeism, and Islam): again I hope they provide useful, amusing or forward-looking perspectives. I should add that some poems first appeared in 'The Rime of the Asian Highway'.

The two fables involving Lord Byron and The Beatles are oblique commentaries on Afghanistan and Russia's war on Ukraine, invoking firstly a world-weary hero who gave his life for a nation's independence, and then the soft-power forces of Freedom that dictators, despite their power, actually fear. And the conclusion is partly drawn from my own experience as part of a 'diasporic' family, focusing on the human reality of today's dispersed lives.

I would like to thank my wife Premila for her support and patience, to Robin Stewart for the cover photograph (taken a few years ago, it must be said) and also to Marion Eastwood of the Oxford Poetry Circle where many of these poems have been aired. If they have a unity it is perhaps suggested by the cover's background, its theme of light and shade a visual suggestion that life is nuanced and complex, rather than black and white.

John Webster, 2025

Contents

TIES OF THE HEART

- 1   A Gallant Ship
- 2   For a Godson
- 5   For Benjamin
- 8   The Major, his brother, and his never lived-with lover
- 9   John Martyn encountered
- 10   Is There a Sense?
- 11   Mary and the Legacy
- 14   For Mark

LIFT-OFFS

- 17   The Plane was Late
- 17   From the Skies
- 18   For Jenny and Chris, *en route* to Nice
- 19   The Dying Glacier
- 20   Thank You, Fog the Second
- 21   Stonehaven
- 22   Aberdeen: Byron's Broad Street boyhood
- 25   'Beatles Ashram', Rishikesh
- 26   Somewhere in this City
- 27   Chennai: 'When I checked in for dental health'
- 28   When there is an Onion Shortage
- 29   The Weightiest Places I Have Been
- 29   Ancestral Skulls: Nairobi National Museum
- 33   'Lerici is Always Charming'
- 34   Thank You … To Who?

WORDS ON THE WOKE

- 37   It's a Woke World … Hurray!
- 38   Apropos 'Appropriation'
- 39   There was a time our own Sir Keir
- 42   On the Return of Donald Trump
- 44   Black Lives Matter (said Lord Bentinck)
- 46   Don't think Black, don't think White
- 47   And on the Mighty Orientalists

NO SUCH THING AS INFIDEL
- 53   The Ballad of Akbar and Aurangzeb
- 54   If Stratford Could Speak
- 55   The Cross and Crescent Wreathed in Flight
- 56   Lebanese Girl Poem
- 56   On Shafilea Ahmed
- 57   An Incident in Peshawar
- 61   These Baklava On My Plate (I Sing of Bad Theology)
- 65   A Poem for Gaza's Young
- 66   A Praise Song

STANZAS ON UKRAINE
- 69   From 1968 to 2022…
- 71   What Gives You the Right?
- 73   Law No More
- 75   He's Just a Common Thief
- 77   Ukraine Dreamin'
- 79   …and on to 2025

81 A BYRONIC FABLE
    In which Lord Byron and Joe Biden reflect on Afghanistan and Greece

87 A BEATLES FABLE
    In which Hitler has a nightmare about a Yellow Submarine

FORWARD THINKING
- 93   The Rise of Diasporic Lives
- 95   For Those Unborn
- 95   A Maxim: All I Can Do

97 NOTES, REFERENCES AND PHOTOGRAPHS

Ties of the heart

A Gallant Ship

A gallant ship is overcome, and cast upon the shore,
Is she broken into pieces, or can she sail once more?
Her flotilla is dumbfounded, she had been so strong,
Battered by the rip tides, always ploughing bravely on.

Watching out for those around, keeping them in shape,
They had not fully realised the toll that it would take;
And building, launching dinghies small to set out on the tides,
Which now look on their mother ship afraid and mystified.

From the start in stormy seas with ballast unsecured,
Hidden deep in secret holds, so hard to find the cause,
And stow them fast and tightly, but she had tried to learn,
Until an overwhelming wave her efforts overturned.

But look, now there is movement, some movement on the shore,
And not a pirate party to wreak destruction more,
But shipbuilders and carpenters and architects marine,
To find the hidden failings and relaunch the gallant Queen.

So her flotilla looks on now, and groups, its strength to fill,
Wishing them the greatest luck and hoping that their skill,
Will help restore her back to them to sail the seven seas,
And she can find her balance and rejoin them at their need.

And to their efforts they can add that very special glue,
That binds, repairs, refastens, and magically renews,
Bringing peace, assurance in their association proud,
So they can all set sail once more and face the darkest cloud.

For a Godson

My Dad he had a godson
Who'd never felt complete:
He'd drifted in and out of things,
And never found his feet.

Now there are those at age of twelve
Who know the way ahead,
Whose life is mapped and from that point,
The path ahead is set.

But he had never been like that,
By his own heart had sailed,
And never met companion true,
To join him on his trail.

But maybe in his fifth decade
A girlfriend he had found,
Who'd touched him to his very soul
And wrought a change profound.

For now he'd found his place in life
And knew the way to go,
A peace had quelled his restless ways
And set him on his road.

And in this new and settled mood
They'd both set off for France,
With friends as well so in a group
To drink and sing and dance.

One afternoon, a peaceful lake
Suggesting, yes, a swim,
In fact to reach the other side
With others he'd jumped in.

They'd got right to the other side
And rested on the shore,
Then set off out to make it back
With no one thinking more…

But halfway back and with his friends
His swimming ceased to be,
There was a sudden stillness
All focussed on that scene.

His heart had stopped and never more
A breath for him to take,
As his lady friend watched on
In the centre of the lake.

You might well call him happy
To die in friendship's fold,
At peace because his light of soul
Had given him a home.

Well my father aged of 89
Sat down to write to her,
Express his thoughts by marsh's side
Some comfort to transfer.

But halfway down the white white page
His pen it faltered, slowed,
He took himself off to his bed
His full thoughts undisclosed.

And from that bed he rose no more
And took his final breath,
And dignified and quietly
He rendezvous'd with death.

And that's the way goddammit
We all should end our days,
Working to the very end,
And thinking of the ways

We can console and be a rock,
To those in loss and pain,
Thinking out for others,
So they can smile again.

For Benjamin

There was no one quite like Benjamin,
No one who can fill his shoes;
Which by the way were leather-free,
In keeping with his views.

I heard that in the playground,
By schoolmates left alone,
He talked to cats, he talked to bees
To join with Nature's flow.

It was the age of ignorance,
By countless actions shown,
But he finessed the bitterness
Which could from that have grown.

So when from school returning,
'Go home' cried out some fool,
'That's what I'm doing' he replied,
Disarmed him with his cool.

And when his young man's world went wrong,
He found a way to go,
Which left those lesser ways behind,
Through verse new worlds he'd know.

The quick wit and the energy,
The Caribbean cool,
His ceaseless work and social grace,
The rhymes that he renewed

Would bring him to the media world,
To radio, book and film,
He'd have to get a hotel suite,
To pack the journos in.

Then when he met with Lady Di,
And didn't want to fart,
In poetry he told the tale,
Which made the country laugh.

A national treasure he became,
Except 'The Sun' was cross,
But in his rhyme 'The Blinding Sun'
He showed them who was boss.

He lent me his celebrity,
For the poet Shelley's sake,
Who he loved, in awe of how
He'd tried so hard to wake

The country from its slumber deep,
And tell the skylark's song;
Invoke in words the Wild West Wind,
His inner fire lifelong.

And the first time he arrived,
He'd just wowed them at Hay,
The second time a hospital ward
Had been honoured with his name.

Then at Brookes when recognized
For making poetry real,
He asked me and my son along
To the celebration meal.

And in old Maxwell's dining room,
Vegan vichyssoise there served,
He just was so engaged with all
While I the guest observed.

I got him on his mobile phone,
The message left was cool:
'I'm probably in the local nick,
In prison or in school'.

Then, I was working, with my mind
So many miles away,
Far off I heard an anguished cry
And next heard my wife say:

That Benjamin had died they'd said,
And nothing to be done;
A brain tumour, a brain tumour,
'Oh no, oh no', so young.

Like so many we were stunned
This source of courage lost;
Those unstraightforward takes on life
That put new twists across.

I looked next day and in 'The Sun'
The tributes all flowed fast;
The times had changed, his deeds had left
Their battles in the past.

Hail to thee, blithe Benjamin!
Hail to your mercury mind;
Thanks for the way you worked for us
And always sought to find

A way to navigate dead ends,
See injustices transformed;
Hail to thee, blithe Benjamin!
May your spirit long go on.

The Major, his brother, and his never lived-with lover

The brother is the historian E.P. Thompson, the 'never lived-with lover' is Iris Murdoch, and the Major is Frank Thompson, the soldier and poet who was executed in Bulgaria in 1944. Inspired by 'A Very English Hero: The Making of Frank Thompson' by Peter Conradi.

There is a story, that when he came to die,
A swirl of glowing fireflies arose before his eye;
A final gift of wonder, of gentleness and peace,
To rebuke his brutal torturers and ease his life's release.

The soldiers in the party, would say they'd aimed to miss,
When they went through his possessions, the evidence was this:
Of a man who'd loved their country, their language and their folk;
Who'd thought of nothing else but helping them to slip their yoke.

I'm thinking of his brother, the historian EP,
And how this must have changed his life – been with him constantly;
I met him once at Glastonbury, after he'd been up on stage:
An electric, rangy figure, depth and passion in his rage.

I asked him about poetry, and think I got this right,
He smiled and said he went with Blake – then disappeared from sight!
His brother was a poet too, so in the realms of verse,
He found perhaps some solace that could help the grief disperse.

And Iris Murdoch thought of him, it's guessed, when she would come to write,
On the persistence of true goodness, when faced with blackest night;
So let that thought survive him, with a forerunner's refrain:
But, you know, that 'I have lived, and have not lived in vain'.

John Martyn encountered

A man of vital paradox, a rugby player at school,
A face of hippie wistfulness with another visage duelled;
Growling, moaning, vocalising from some hurt inside,
Honest beyond honesty with nothing feared to hide.

Waves of sound sent crashing out, just one man with guitar,
Rocking backwards in his chair, entranced in world afar;
Fingers flying, slapping, climbing, notes many or few,
Cascading layers of pulsing sound sent washing over you.

And then he laughs, and makes a joke and throws it all away,
Shows he's human after all, the tension then assuaged;
Held the hall right in his hands his power to unify,
And then a song that gently touches everyone inside.

'Oh John had demons' said his friend who'd played with him in clubs,
His manager advancing wads of cash for damages to pubs;
His wife a troubled history to speak of in their lives,
Friends' faraway expressions when this they tried to clarify.

Part Glaswegian hard man, part Home Counties soft,
Childhood letters to his Mum with heart-breaking sense of loss;
And yet the cards dealt out to him he played as best he could,
A tolerant compassion kindness twisting through his roots.

And here he was in Nottingham, and being the main man,
His presence helping raise some funds for some youthful fans;
Absolutely there for them in all complexity,
And here straightforward giving out with no tricks up his sleeve.

Finishing with 'Solid Air' he held the room transfixed,
Pride in his unique quality – 'no one taught me this'!
A song for his true friend Nick Drake, for whom he deeply cared,
And backstage in the dressing room, he spoke with music there.

Is There a Sense?

'Mahatma Gandhi and Martin Luther King are great examples of fantastic nonviolents who died violently, I can never work that out. We're pacifists, but I'm not sure what it means when you're such a pacifist that you get shot. I can never understand that'.
(John Lennon, 1980)

Is there a sense
That some people get
Too big for this world we inhabit?

That if they went on
With their art or their song
It would somehow disorder the planet?

We can all of us think
Of those who would drink
Of a spring that's not given to all

With beauty and danger
Combined in its flows
Casting spells that cannot be ignored.

Why else would the great
Whose path and whose fate
Had led to an unspeakable fall

Be taken from life
By gun or by knife
In scenes that perplex and appal?

Mary and the Legacy

Now these books upon my bookshelf tell a tale that must be told,
On the left in covers plain, on the right in green and gold;
To the left a thicker volume, that's of slightly later date,
All tokens of a story of devotion I'll relate.

It's of a grieving widow poring over the remains
Of her husband's stellar output, by censorship still chained;
She'd managed to get something out, but not his complete work,
His own father had suppressed it, that publication first.

So you can see, there seemed to be, more than a bit at stake,
Just what had got his father's goat to make him so irate?
Where to begin? ... the politics, love over property,
His class betrayal, atheism, love of liberty.

But that was 1824, now fifteen years have gone,
His father's threats have lost their power, and she has seized upon
The opportunity to print once more ... why the whole damn thing,
With recollections of his life strategically thrown in.

So this will be the first real time, that the world can see,
Her husband's full achievements, in their entirety;
Into the nineteenth century dropped this prime poetic prize,
His detractors needing weapons new to bring him down to size.

One poem still a sticking point for the establishment,
Minds legal and religious to 'Queen Mab' will be bent;
'A youthful folly', they will say, though those dreaming of life new
Had published it in pirate form, and revealed the poet's view

Of the life transformed he told of, and through the Faery Queen,
Who rode her magic chariot above the aery sheen
Of the earth's cradling atmosphere, ascending high and free
Showing what has been, and is, that need not always be.

So the law of libel blasphemous has been for long employed,
Against the pirate publishers and the readers they enjoyed,
But Mary has a publisher in high society,
So when *he* prints Shelley's poems, he should from pains be free.

And yet when the new edition, at last would see the light,
'Queen Mab' had been truncated, its omission was a blight;
Mary wanted Shelley's work to its widest audience find,
And thought 'Mab' to his merits would make his readers blind.

But there were bitter protests made: 'So why's 'Queen Mab' not here'?
Mary and Moxon then would print it full, later in the year;
'At my request', Mary would write, 'the publisher's agreed,
To restore the omitted passages and so his work is now complete'.

And then there was another twist, because another publisher saw,
A chance to challenge those who long had plagued him through the law;
He'd gone to prison many times and pirated 'Queen Mab',
And thought: 'through this I'll try to get those bastards off my back!'

'To maybe even end, for good, that blasphemous libel rule,
 I'll launch a case myself, so I can show the law's a fool,
'Queen Mab', I will allege in court, is of great blasphemy,
Profane, offensive, egregious, yes, in its impiety…

'But hope it will be cleared of all such accusations fake,
So no one in the future can those allegations make;
And the fact that it's been published by a publisher so fine,
Will help my cause immensely, they'll see him as benign'.

And so, at last, the day did dawn when 'Queen Mab' came to trial,
With Mary watching from afar, and taking Moxon's side,
Up rose the prosecution, with their rhetoric intense,
On how 'Queen Mab' would cause to all immeasurable offence.

'No no', replied stout Talfourd, 'It is a flight of fancy free,
And a noble work of literature, which must defended be',
But all his counter-rhetoric convinced the jury not
Within a quarter of an hour they a guilty verdict dropped.

But Hetherington, the publisher, would not the judgement force,
And no one had the appetite to pursue the matter more;
So 'Queen Mab's publication then would never more be blocked,
And the 'Society for Suppressing Vice' within five years was stopped.

For Mary this whole saga was a matter of the heart,
A message to her husband lost that she would take his part:
First deciphering, and copying out his handwriting so wild,
Then collecting, arranging, titling, in volumes four compiled.

And on my shelf these volumes sit, both testaments to love,
And showing too how Freedom, can hurdles rise above;
And here's a thought, just come to mind, if she had drownéd been
With Shelley, in that shipwreck, how would his work be seen?

For Mark

Hey my friend, you've had to leave us,
Hey my friend, you've had to go,
Back in primary school I knew you:
We then travelled friendship's road.

I don't know, we just were buddies,
Then the music came along,
We drifted through each other's houses,
Shared a secret world of song.

Coming back from Bardney festival,
You tripped headlong on a tent;
Flattened it beyond redemption,
Oops a daisy – off we went.

Though our paths were then diverted,
An outlook shared kept coming back;
Lincoln summers, autumns, winters
Smoking fags by racecourse track.

Then we'd meet again in London,
In your convivial Fulham home;
Parties, laughs, goodhearted friends
Latest sounds and rock 'n' roll.

And if confusions, ills descended;
On your family or friend,
Steadfast succour you extended,
Their life and being to defend.

And when my wife by magic met me,
You were for her a truest friend;
Sharing jokes and joint perspectives,
Test match texts to type and send.

And then there was your lovely wedding:
Good Karma sure had come for good,
In a classic English setting,
We rejoiced as there you stood.

And next Big Oil would lose its purchase,
Farming power from the wind,
From your Isle of Wight old rectory,
Beloved daughter now within.

We walked to the beach together,
Cliff and bonfire under moon,
You played Tom Waits into the evening,
And after that only the phone.

Macca's song about Picasso,
Was playing when I heard the news,
I then played Tom Traubert's blues song,
So it could with your spirit fuse.

Hey my friend, you've had to leave us:
The world will never be the same;
And yet your presence in the present
Will light up when we speak your name.

Lift-offs

The Plane was Late

The plane was late when we departed
And so the airline's word was broken
We'd tried our best to stay stout-hearted
Hoping it was just a token
Of a thing that could not last
But soon be banished to the past.
And so it proved, and we were off
And at our former fears did scoff.

From the Skies

The habitations of the globe
In diamond lights pass by below
In those individual worlds
Panoplies of life unfurl
And the children brought to light
Gaze and smile on each new sight
Taking what they see as given
Until their childhood minds are riven
Then their wills awake to strive
And bring new ways to be alive
Fresh realms uncovered and then nourished
In which succeeding offspring flourish.

For Jenny and Chris, *en route* to Nice

It is nice to be in Nice,
To be in Nice is nice;
So should you get the chance to go
You won't have to think twice.

There is water from the hills,
The sea is sparkling blue,
And from the Promenade des Anglais
You'll get a marvellous view.

In springtime it is temperate,
Though there could be some rain,
And if there is a thunderstorm
We'll need Matisse again.

Then when the streets have been washed down,
And all the air is clear,
To re-enjoy their peerless home
The Niçois will appear.

Then it is nice to be in Nice,
To be in Nice is nice;
So should you get the chance to go
You won't have to think twice!

The Dying Glacier

The melancholy glacier,
Its former glory late,
With a blue and patient eye
Looks out upon its fate.

A tear is running down its cheek
On bare uncovered ground,
A rivulet that's running fast
Where once its ice was found.

Like a beast who knows its time is up,
The slaughterhouse is near,
But cannot voice its warnings shrill
Or tell its inner fears.

And we who are there witnessing
That noble thing expire,
In what's a devil's paradox
Add to its funeral pyre.

We thought that we had long outgrown
Those old religious dreads,
But nurtured by our modern world
New fears have grown instead.

Maybe the planes will miss the towers,
Maybe a plan be found,
To remove destructive greenhouse gas
And turn that process round

And then though it will centuries take
Our friend could slowly grow,
And take its place on mountain side
No more its tears will flow.

But that is surely looking through
A wishful thinking scope,
Yet as dear Woody Guthrie said,
All Man can do is hope.

Thank You, Fog the Second

One morn in rural England's clasp
And as a mist arose,
'Thank you, fog' the poet thought
As over him it closed.

For cut off in a manor house,
Surrounded by his friends,
He was separated from the world
And its woes that never end.

In Patagonia's landscape wild
Where we were out at large,
My iPhone failed, my watch gave out,
My tablet would not charge.

It was like a fog descended
Just like in Auden's day,
Surrounded too with friendship's balm
While the world went on its way.

Scotland: Stonehaven

Weathered cliffs and rounded bays,
Washed by ever-breaking waves,
Above the sound of seagulls shrill,
Breezes warm with edge of chill.

The harbour seen from high descent,
Boats rest tethered, storms long spent,
And there sprinkled round the edge
Hostelries their care dispense.

Enjoyed by those from near and far,
Fare from restaurants, bistros, bars,
All enhanced by memories
Of matchless views, pleasant fatigue.

So 'hey that was a castle true,
Standing in exquisite view,
A castle that justified itself
Protecting a nation's rightful wealth.

And yet it seems some things occurred
That now would tell of morals blurred,
So history's complicated track
From simple judgements bring one back'.

And up on high the temple to
The dead from World Wars One and Two;
Yet at the end these scenes of peace,
May they across the world increase!

Aberdeen:
Byron's Broad Street boyhood

No trace of Byron's boyhood home,
Yet these surrounds he would have known;
Here in Broad Street Aberdeen,
Because his father libertine –

Had made his heiress mother's cash
Disappear in a flash!
But as her kin for her retained
A portion, they the journey made

To Aberdeen, as a retreat,
First in Queen's, then in Broad Street,
Living there in straitened times,
Despite her noble Gordon line.

And then his Dad to see her came –
But really just to money claim;
Their quarrels leaving him bereft,
And then his Dad forever left.

The Greyfriars church he would have seen,
In Back Wynd's passageway have been;
And here he teased his Mum and guests
By throwing out a pillow dressed

In his clothes from window high
While uttering a piercing cry!
What a shock they must have had!
What relief to see the lad!

'Dinna speak of it!' he'd cried,
With little whip he then let fly,
At tactless nurse who had exclaimed:
'So sad this pretty boy is lame'.

And then a mile across the town,
He found his way, with schoolboy frown,
To the school where he began
That learning which the classics spanned.

He'd read of the exotic East,
On tales Arabian he'd feast;
The Old Testament preferred to New,
But poems all he would eschew.

A helper young by name May Gray,
Would 'tricks upon his person' play,
And yet a pious girl was she,
A first taste of hypocrisy.

In fact, in later life he'd say
This early knowledge spoiled his way,
With those pleasures known too young,
His chances of true love undone.

Then one day, when he was ten,
His childhood would mutate again:
To headmaster's study he was called
And told: 'Son, now you are a Lord!'

And given cake and claret fine –
His status by those gifts defined;
Though he would find the tears sprang
At assembly, when his title rang

Around the room, all turned to see
The new Lord Byron – there revealed!
And so to new life he was called
Beyond that academic hall.

But took with him the memories
Of Scotland's beauty, wild, serene;
Recalled from Pisa's study room,
Where his remembrances would bloom

In that palazzo there immersed,
Recalling Scotland's soul in verse,
A late recall before he'd part,
The call of Greece a burning spark,

That would grow into a flame,
That burned all his old life away:
From women, poet's fame enticed
For Missolonghi's sacrifice.

O ye in Broad Street Aberdeen,
Think of him who here has been!

'Beatles Ashram', Rishikesh, 2014

From this source of purest song,
Near where a myth-bound river flows;
In the hollows of the hills,
Came William and his Bungalow.

'Dear Prudence' she was here,
In her quarters she did hide;
'Sexy Sadie' came to light,
From a trusting, then sardonic mind.

Monkeys mating in the dust—
'Why Don't We Do It In The Road?';
'Piggies' clutching forks and knives,
In their dinner clothes.

And the Queen of all the brood,
Those 'airy children of the brain';
'Julia', that floating spell,
That told of loss, but also gain.

For days I stayed some miles away,
Even at that distance feeling blessed;
The landscape that I looked out on,
With wit and beauty still impressed.

Somewhere in This City

Somewhere in this city
Is a boy whose life has changed,
Somewhere a loving mother
Who will never more be found;
Only three years old
He knows he'll never see her more,
For yesterday they laid her in the ground.

Let us hope that boy will now
Be gifted kindness as he grows,
And finds some constant caring
From his own community;
Let's wish on him a loving wife
And children of his own
To make his own supporting family.

It's hard to feel that absence though
That sometimes will appear,
In the morning, night, at mealtimes,
Or in sudden playground tears;
Can we hope it will be balanced
By a type of growing strength
That will then serve to sustain him through the years?

Chennai: When I Checked in for Dental Health

When I checked in for dental health
The neon Buddha on the shelf
Gave off a reassuring air
As I settled in the chair
As if through all I could relax
And meditate right to the max
And think how fortunate we are
That ages rude have faded far
And now we live in better times
Which anaesthetics have refined
So now those quite undreamed-of pains
Long-lasting aches so near the brain
Are largely left far in the past
By scientific minds outcast.

And so it proved, for even the
Usual injection preliminary
Was eased with anaesthetic spray
I hardly felt it make its way
And then I sat there looking on
At the Buddha in neon.

As a specialist did his work
My wife there to the dentist talked
And saw photos of some folk he'd treated
Rebuilt their jaws by paan depleted
One side fully eaten away
By vicious juices there decayed
Disfigured, and so hard to swallow
To hide inside no life to follow.
With silicon he had rebuilt
The absent tissue to the hilt
Through his skills he there did seek
To reinstate the missing cheek.

Before and after, what a sight
The sad and ugly there made right
'I don't charge them' he softly said
'If they can't afford their daily bread'.

The neon Buddha seemed to glow
More brightly as his tale he told
Compassion's essence living on
Championed in his age bygone.

And I got up out of the chair
I hardly knew that I'd been there….

When There is an Onion Shortage

When there is an onion shortage
India is so on edge!
It's downright existential:
The politicians rush to pledge

That 'action fast will soon be taken,
Imports aren't ruled out,
Soon things will return to rule,
There'll be no more onion drought.

No, no more dearth or scarcity,
There'll be a glut in fact;
Because we know we will be gone
If you haven't seen us act!'

The Weightiest Places

The weightiest places I have been,
Are those which have past conflict seen,
Which have seen foes at daggers drawn,
But now exist in peace reborn.

There was the Vietnam hotel,
Where war had cast its malign spell,
In Hué, by the riverside,
By a bridge that crossed its moving tide.

Across the bridge was Hué's old city,
Where the Viet Cong were sitting pretty,
Inside the massive citadel,
And all were deep in war's own hell.

Our hotel was white and spacious,
A restful old colonial dream,
At breakfast there were omelette stations,
The staff in whites all pressed and clean.

And with smiles that were not faked,
Youngsters starting out in life;
Unlike their parents traumatised
By merciless and vicious strife.

In fact one told us of her grandad —
He'd lived in reeds for seven years;
He could not shake the memories,
With alcohol they dulled his fears.

And outside, just by the bridge,
A spit of land in photo seen,
With mortars lobbed across the river
By a stressed US marine.

Now there are days of peace and commerce,
Now there are days of normal life;
Evenings of convivial company,
Social calm and peaceful nights.

Fast forward now to new Berlin,
Reunited after suffering
The pains of a division deep,
And minefields sown and sorrow reaped.

At Checkpoint Charlie's crossing point
Where tanks lined up when tension grew,
Joke Soviet guards are there to pose
With tourists who line up to view

Those now-mocked, then much-feared guards,
Who there provide an earning chance,
With smiles and laughter generated,
The occasion on the websites rated.

Upon the world's far other side,
I caught my breath when I espied,
A palace low on TV seen,
Where Allende's experiment had been

Crushed by bombs and in that coup,
Had perished there at his own hand;
While the general who'd deceived
Went on to rule that fertile land.

At the spot a statue stands,
Allende's image and last words:
'I have faith in Chile and its future' —
A dream that has in truth occurred.

With the military now off the streets,
The generals banished to their realm,
The government changed by people's votes,
Who get to choose those at the helm.

Those dictatorships, that were so rife,
Upheld in many a short-sighted land;
Now across the continent
On shrinking islands fearful stand.

By Pisa's Solferino bridge,
Our cappuccinos were consumed,
With a pastry too no doubt,
Before our wanderings resumed.

A photo in an exhibition
Showed the city in the War:
That very river wall we'd looked on,
Smashed by shellfire, now restored.

A Sherman tank with diesel fuming
Was racing fast from left to right,
So purposeful in its mission —
We'd just watched cars at the lights.

Another photo showed the bombers
Up on high above the land;
The city and the wandering Arno,
Held in the earth's enfolding hand.

One more, with buildings on the Arno,
With gaping holes where blown away,
By those unfeeling birds of Freedom,
Released by war to have their day.

One of those gaps was the apartment
Where Mary, Percy Bysshe had been,
I always think whenever I pass it
If only I could inside have seen.

Did his study face the river?
Did he really have that view?
What about their little boy?
Where was their kitchen, and their loo?

But the loss I know is just a small one,
Compared to human tragedies,
That brought sorrow, emptiness
To far too many families.

In these places there is sorrow,
And also a feeling sweet:
That sanity can succeed madness,
Disputes with resolution meet.

Ancestral Skulls: Nairobi National Museum

In the cradle of humanity,
Where our origins are found;
And records of our primal past
Were lifted from the ground

Presented there in standing case
The skulls which show just how
The adaptations had occurred
To cheek, to skull, to brow

Which led to that capacious brain
The home of human mind,
Which now explores the universe
Its ambitions unconfined.

Italy: 'Lerici is Always Charming'

'Lerici is always charming', said Elisa at the desk,
Of our hotel, when we were leaving,
And our stay had sure impressed:
Our room that looked on 'Shelley's view',
The castle and the curving bay,
The walkway, great for people watching,
As they made their different ways

From San Terenzo to Lerici, and the town's endearing space:
Pine trees by the promenade,
With restaurants, bistros, all there placed;
People on the ferries starting, looking out across the bay,
Sunhats on in late September, suspended in the journey's sway.

Or from Lerici to San Terenzo,
Which D.H. Lawrence called sublime,
Its beauty such, it almost hurt to see, it was so fine;
And with the spirit of Virginia, there to Mary Shelley feel,
A kindred spirit with her burdens; the Casa Magni there to steal

One's thoughts to Jane upon the balcony,
Guitar notes taking Shelley's heart
Away from Mary, into verses, touched with regrets that life imparts;
And all those dramas of their stay
With strange outbursts of psychic force,
Widows waiting for the sail, but both undone by death's pale horse.

And after nightfall, when the moon shone,
Just like then across the bay,
Silver light upon the water, starlight adding to its play,
Portovenere in the distance, with memories of time well spent,
Lerici, we will return, that is for sure our firm intent!

Thank You ... To Who?

Thank you for our planet home,
This space in which we live and breathe,
Thank you to ... a Principle?
Of life beyond us to conceive?

We may think a loving presence
Is beyond what sense can bear,
The cosmos may be enigmatic,
And yet we see precision there.

For we can see that there is order,
Reflected in a spokéd wheel,
The rule of law, the working world,
The natural justice that we feel.

There is also generation,
Nature ever pushing through,
Natural beings renovating,
Growing into something new.

Originating at the outset,
Expanding outwards into space,
Through matter giving berthing platforms,
Including for our human race.

And then as well there is profusion,
Ever grouping into types:
Species, patterns, mathematics,
The sunflower head, the zebra's stripes.

There is too rolling refinement,
A pull to move on and perfect,
That drives the engineer's day job,
That lets the expert eye select.

Yet to this world of perfect order,
Other things have entered in:
Those faults genetic, sad but natural
The urgings towards a thoughtless sin.

For 'All Things Bright and Beautiful'
Was by the Pythons satirized,
With 'All Things Sick and Cancerous'
Part of what we witness live.

Thus Ruin lives within Creation,
Within this Principle of Life,
Which should make us welcome more
Those times when we are free from strife

And set off to explore the world
In all its fascinating range,
Indebted to that Principle,
Whatever we may call its name.

Words on the Woke

It's a Woke World ... Hurray!

Right is Left and Left is Right,
Internet is full of spite,
If you're not rocked as fake news trends,
Comments stand your hair on end!

Lady Reason's in a fix,
Now, we're told, she don't exist:
Orwell's banished from the room –
In comes Foucault, za za zoom!

Out goes Churchill, in comes Marx,
Who played the Stock Exchange for larks;
I wonder what sins his stocks entailed?
(I hope Highgate won't be assailed).

And will we ever hear addressed —
The slaves Mohammed sure possessed?
Or of the Arab slave trade long?
Of Chios butchered by Ottoman?

Oh my gosh it's all confused!
What on earth is one to do?
I'll tell you what: think for yourself,
And look at facts and evidence.

And recall the poet's watchword,
That he tossed out so casually:
'Let us see the truth' he wrote,
'The truth whatever it may be' .

Apropos Appropriation

If the electrified guitar
Was invented in America,
Must it then be never played
In those lands it was not made?

What a shame if Fela Kuti
Had been banned from making sounds of beauty;
The music at which McCartney wept:
From that should we be bereft?

No hummus could be made in Chile,
No pizzas anywhere but Italy,
No braided hair in Western lands,
Don't even think of hennaed hands!

Would it be appropriate
Forever to dissociate?
If cultural sharing is appropriation,
That will lessen every nation.

No, it must be inappropriate,
That meaning of … 'appropriate';
Apropos its thoughtless use,
It's inappropriate abuse.

There Was a Time Our Own Sir Keir

There was a time our own Sir Keir
Could not be exactly clear,
About that issue which so perplexes
All – the nature of the sexes.

So 'it was very wrong to say'
The cervix was a female trait,
And on some women – there was a fraction
With a penis there for action.

In fact by his computation
There were 35,000 in the nation,
Of such nature-defying cases:
You should have seen the people's faces!

So some unfriendly rag had fun,
By then outlining, one by one,
Just what his fellow pols did say,
Which it falls to me to now relay:

'Rachel Reeves equivocated,
Did not deny what Keir had stated;
Angie Rayner was oblique,
Thought the debate could damage wreak.

'Pat McFadden hummed and hawed,
Yvette declared she was so bored
With the question asked of her:
Such a distraction she averred!

'Brigitte Phillipson thought that loos
Should be across the genders used,
Lisa Nandy had a spat
With J.K. Rowling – fancy that!

'And Ian Murray…' Ok, who's he?
(The ex-Scottish Secretary actually),
'…Advocated the ejection
Of all who asked an awkward question'.

As that would be discriminatory,
And fatal to equality;
For those who backed a woman's right
Were somehow now all ruled to blight

The brave new world of gender groups
Which had arrived beyond dispute;
Enriching those who, self-assured,
Went far and wide to spread the cause

And act with quite distressing hate
Against the heroines of late:
Once cherished and with countless fans,
Now viewed as being 'anti-trans'.

And because they were now deemed to be
'Feministic trans-exclusionary',
Those in men's bodies now had found
A new way of keeping women down.

And this group formed quite a lobby
With a moral calling (not a hobby),
Who'd taken root on the high ground
And bossed all (including Keir) around.

But lo! from high a judgement came,
A mighty wind, a rushing flame!
For just as we were getting used
To fluid genders – they were traduced

By, no less, the Supreme Court,
Who judged no more should it be thought,
That anyone could themselves declare
Any sex that they now cared.

No, gender was biological,
A judgement wholly logical,
And quite in line with common sense,
(If I may that dated view dispense).

At this Sir Keir was much relieved,
He now knew what he could believe!
In truth he'd known it all along:
(How could the world have got him wrong?)

Of course there might be questions posed,
As to whether this might him expose
As a trimmer who'd give ground
To those who made the loudest sound.

Unlike brave women from the North,
Who grave abuse had long endured,
For stating that a woman's space
Should be protected not displaced.

And spare a thought for one MP,
Who'd stated what the court decreed,
But had been the subject of Keir's wrath
And all the gender lobby's froth.

Rosie Duffield is her name,
Events have shown she's without blame,
But now he's come to take her side
I think he should apologise.

And on that note let's end this story,
Which has not covered all with glory,
And say that if Sir Keir was seized,
With contrition, we'd be pleased.

On the Return of Donald Trump

Many spirits had a slump
With the return of Donald Trump,
But may I play a different role
And perhaps some silver linings show?

There's now no talk of civil war
(Should there have been disputed score);
I know it may be hard to swallow
But dear Kamala he beat hollow.

And it's likely there will be
Less focus on identity;
With all that gender stuff ejected,
Women's sport will be protected.

And, as well, David Lammy finds
He now must eat a humble pie
Of size quite huge, all due to his
Former florid utterances:

'A neo-Nazi, Ku Klux too
A sociopath and tyrant who
Hated women, was a spiv'
(Now all that's 'inoperative')

So J.D. Vance is quite a guy,
His book it even made him cry;
Had lunch with Trump and wasn't shot,
In fact their friendship is now hot!

And so a new and humbler Lammy
Is bound to now materialise;
Making balanced judgements daily,
With wisdom deep he will surprise.

And when he mounts his moral horse,
He'll restrain, for sure, his grand discourse.
For, as could have been expected,
On his past he'll have reflected.

Black Lives Matter (said Lord Bentinck)

'Black Lives Matter', said Lord Bentinck,
As he saw the mourners bring,
A woman to her husband's funeral —
There to feel the flames' sharp sting.

Then the pain so incandescent
With its rage beyond control,
Would give its pang of recognition:
'This funeral pyre will take my soul'.

'Black Lives Matter', said Lord Bentinck,
This practice cannot be just,
To burn live wives with husbands' corpses
You must this practice now adjust'.

'But Sir, this is our settled custom'
Said the men of priestly caste;
'Widows burn at husbands' funerals,
To change this now you cannot ask'.

'Well we too have a little custom',
Replied Lord Bentinck, 'for those men,
Who murder women through this practice' –
And those high-castes listened then.

'I have to tell you' said Lord Bentinck,
'That it is a custom grim:
Carpenters will build a gallows,
And there those murderers will swing'.

For 'Black Lives Matter', said Lord Bentinck,
'Black Lives Matter', said the Law;
'Black Lives Matter', said the Parliament,
Backing Bentinck to the core.

'But Sir', the righteous of our era,
Say with truly puzzled mien,
'Colonists are always wicked,
That is now by all agreed'.

'So saving lives of helpless women,
We can't believe this you did do,
That would just be too ironic,
A thing that we could not compute'.

'So please, oh please, my dear Lord Bentinck,
Do not with irony overload,
Our poor heads, they cannot stand it
They will undoubtedly explode!

'For we indeed say 'Black Lives Matter',
But only black lives in the zone,
Of our righteous indignation,
Beyond that anything will go'.

'In the end', so says this writer,
'Careful judgement must be made;
The gallows for the Freedom Fighters,
Set against the widows saved.

'Who numbered 20,000 yearly
By some estimates I have seen;
So please don't say that all is simple
In face of History's ironies'.

Don't think Black, don't think White.

Don't think Black, think Unfaded,
White should just be Faded rated;
'BAME'* is lame and bureaucratic,
A view of folk divisive, static.

After all, at human dawn,
Dark skin would protect from harm;
When some moved to northern climes,
Their black pigment did decline.

Otherwise the vitamins,
Partly admitted through their skins,
Would be seriously deficient—
Isn't Nature so efficient?

Divide us not by skin colour,
Difference comes from money, culture,
Not to mention geography,
Which distributes unequally.

So don't think Black, think Unfaded,
White should just be Faded rated;
Don't resort to that word 'BAME' —
In human terms we're all the same!

*'Black, Asian and Minority Ethnic'

And on the Mighty Orientalists

Remember how there was a heyday
Of the Mighty Orientalists?
Led by Said, who had his points,
But never once a chance would miss

To both play down and denigrate,
The scholars, artists, writers who,
Would travel into Orient lands,
And seek to ignorance undo.

For he saw lurking in their efforts,
A hidden hand of malign power;
That was in fact their whole core purpose,
Just servants of the ruler's hour.

But is there harm in curious questing?
In seeking truths in foreign lands?
Collecting, studying, codifying,
With cultures deepened by their hands?

For if these practices are frowned on
How I ask should one proceed?
The impulse would be to isolate,
And miss the other's strengths and needs.

Did he speak for the complacent
Those satisfied by things that be?
To rest within a settled culture,
With no shred of curiosity.

Just like that Ottomanic Sultan
One book translated in his reign:
Of pure self-interest, how to cure
The curse of syphilitic pains.

With the whole enlightening project,
Initiated in the West,
Damned as some mere power play –
Did not, in fact, it serve to bless

The human race with its enhancements,
Many in truth of Scottish birth;
For 'no small land apart from Greece
Ever gave more to planet earth'.

So said Winston Churchill truly,
I had a tea towel once that said the same,
It listed every great attainment
Achieved under a Scottish name.

So every time you drive on tarmac,
With a tyre that bears the car;
Each day you turn on the telly,
Or demand a fried Mars bar –

Remember Scotland! This list stretches
Far ahead and out of sight,
But as I write on Edward Said,
I must not let its telling blight

This work and its intrinsic something,
Nor raise its cost in printers' ink,
That costs far more than fine champagne,
And that's a fact on which to think.

So I'll conclude with two reflections,
The first upon Sir William Jones;
From Wales he was and in Calcutta
Found Indian culture in his bones.

He formed a learned coterie,
And from his mind the volumes poured,
On Hindu and Islamic cultures,
And on their languages and Laws.

(And his motive for the latter
Was to that tradition save,
He'd heard Salafists and Wahabis
Were throwing learning on the flames).

And two hundred years on,
He was honoured, for his field
Of Hindu and Islamic studies,
And how old India he'd revealed.

All organised by local scholars,
And that must surely go to show,
That people from a once-colonised country
Can see those guys could help them grow.

And so, in spite of all the bad stuff,
The baby in the tub should stay,
And there is value in such work,
Despite what Edward Said might say.

Said himself has had his critics,
Of his scholarship, and also whether,
He'd falsified his background story,
And glibly linked too much together.

But secondly, there's one fine memory,
A highly admirable act:
His founding of an orchestra,
With the Jewish Barenboim in fact.

For that was to boost understanding
Between the Arab and the Jew;
And from musicians far and wide
Who came to them – on them they drew

And it continues to the present,
Each year a summer school in Spain,
Performances from Prague to Chengdu,
Where its other vision reigns.

So if his book has been contested,
Yet now with much seen in its light,
His and Daniel's music ensemble
Carries on with purpose bright.

No Such Thing as Infidel

The Ballad of Akbar and Aurangzeb

Have you heard of Akbar and Aurangzeb?
And their oh-so-different ways?
Rulers of the Moghul Empire,
In India, and surviving to this day.

Akbar, he was a Sufi thinker,
Delighting in arcane philosophy;
With Hindus, Buddhists, Christians he would talk,
About the world and life's great mysteries.

Aurangzeb ruled generations later,
He murdered his brothers for the throne;
He outlawed music and performance,
And tore down Hindu temples stone by stone.

Akbar believed in freedom of religion:
Reason, said he, must be supreme;
And that hallowed region of tradition,
Should not be as a long-term prison seen.

Aurangzeb you know he was quite different,
He ordered Christian priests to be enslaved;
He also beheaded a Guru of the Sikhs,
Because Islam he refused to embrace.

Now Akbar had abolished,
The jizya tax non-Muslims had to pay;
Guess what, Aurangzeb, he re-imposed it,
So infidels were kept under his sway.

Now the future must be with Muslims like Akbar,
In our world of the coming century;
And let's hope that Aurangzebi Muslims
Can find a way to love humanity.

Have you heard of Akbar and Aurangzeb?
They're still surviving to this day.

If Stratford Could Speak

As a teenager Osama bin Laden visited Shakespeare's birthplace, writing later: 'We went every Sunday to visit Shakespeare's house. I was not impressed and I saw that they were a society different from ours and that they were a morally loose society'. At which point, a mighty voice, seeming to rise from the town's streets, theatres, buildings and very air, was mysteriously heard:

'Shall I compare thee to the Ku Klux Klan?
Thou art as brutish and untaught:
From the depth of thy dull heart,
All balance, empathy long gone,
You seek to force your narrow thought.

For us, years past, we grew through this,
And brought about a social code
Where fierce convictions could co-exist,
Enabled, checked, by rule of law.
And then, with love and hatred twined,
We fought your Nazi friends to dust,
From which the flower of Freedom grew.

While you may cause us sacrifice,
We will do the same for you.

Oh, and we must quote The Bard,
Quote him from his Twelfth Night tale:

'Dost thou think, because thou art 'virtuous',
There shall be no more cakes and ale?'

The Cross and Crescent Wreathed in Flight

The words were carefully chosen,
And have lasted into time:
'Give to Caesar what is his,
Put God's share to one side'.

And that would set a paradigm,
Where each would have their space,
They'd jockey for position, sure,
But mostly now the State

In the present takes the lead,
And must adjudicate,
The living stream of living lives
Where each to all relate.

Yet there's a different paradigm,
That's in a different book,
Which centuries later would be writ
And a whole new claim it took:

It should command all earthly things,
And be the rule for Man,
And *it* was God, the book itself,
And should all existence span.

So in the book, when claims are made,
Believers must agree,
Their entire lives be organised
By what that book decrees.

It is the highest authority
And overrides the State,
And there are many negatives
Which draw believers in their wake.

Not all believers, no of course
Most find the positives,
Those which enable harmony,
Let them with others live.

Their natural human instincts too,
The need to live and thrive,
Make them ignore those low-down thoughts
And in some mental storeroom hive.

Perhaps just like those Bible lines
In which a vengeful God paraded,
But now in mainstream Christian minds
Have just into the background faded.

And scholars work their ways around
Whenever there are rulings cruel;
Invoke the context of their age,
And finesse them in the new.

But, there is no one authority
To say: 'This is the Law',
So any half-baked psychopath
Can rise and take the floor

And say: 'Here is the Word of God
Which you should all obey,
And those lines about the 'infidel'
That's what God himself does say'.

So it is not straightforward,
As countless things have shown,
For followers in the Western world
Where that two-fold path has grown.

And in truth, though every effort
Must be made to educate,
These new arrivals in our lands
To the basis of the State

And pay regard to what is said
Where're the book holds sway,
And draw the line at bad doctrine
Which can lead lives astray

We'll never be able to stamp out
That narrow-minded view:
Sadly it will e'er recur,
With sorrow rising new.

For there is no one authority
To say: 'This is the Law',
So any half-baked psychopath
Can rise and take the floor

And say: 'Here is the Word of God
Which you should all obey,
And those lines about the 'infidel'
That's what God himself does say'.

Lebanese Girl Poem

There's something wrong, so very wrong, when an eight year old,
Is locked away and beaten because her parents had been told,
She'd taken off her hijab that afternoon at school,
I guess it was quite hot that day, she wanted to be cool.

And then her head shaved, what a thing to inflict on your child,
Pure abuse, but by a mindset fully justified;
But a mindset under pressure, you sense the insecurity,
That comes from Arab women who are wanting to break free.

And locked up in a cupboard too with no refuge in Law,
Not one shred of compassion from the two who brought her forth,
I hope, young lady, you will find, when they are both no more,
Your own way and your freedom, with your mind and life unscored.

On Shafilea Ahmed

Now to my mind comes Shafilea Ahmed,
Who of a lawyer's life did dream,
But pledged in marriage by her parents,
They murdered her at 17.

The judge declared their expectation,
That Shafilea's life would fuel,
Some godforsaken foreign land deal,
Was unrealistic, toxic, cruel.

They'll be in prison till the thirties,
Unlikely to admit their wrong,
With minds closed to tropes of freedom,
Hoping that their world grows strong.

With the wide world there for taking,
But not one thought of input making,
Let time wash such mindsets away,
Awakening to the light of day.

An Incident in Peshawar

An excerpt from 'The Rime of the Asian Highway', revealing how little agency women have in Muslim cultures, and commenting on the the response to grooming gangs in the UK.

For as we set off, packs on back, to find the edge of town,
A smartly dressed man then appeared, politely flagged us down;
'Would we like some chai'? he asked – 'Well sure that would be good',
He found for us a little shop and chai appeared – with food.

And he produced a wad of notes and turned his face to me,
A proposition then was made which I realised gradually
Was not altogether decent, in fact, quite the opposite:
He hoped that I would take the cash and authorise a tryst

Between him and my partner who was sitting there bemused,
He didn't even look at her or conceive she could refuse!
The meet it grew in import as events and years went by,
A real and lived experience which to issues grave applied.

So later, when the penny dropped, I began to understand,
A woman was the property, the chattel of the man.
He'd thought her at my sole command, for me to use at will,
And earn myself some rupees too if that would give a thrill.

So now, as we are on the brink of leaving Muslim lands,
Let me put my thoughts in order and try to understand
The true nature of this mindset and how it operates,
And works in our society and to the world relates.

For everyone is mixed up now and trying to get on,
To understand how cultures work: that surely can't be wrong.
So if I take some time and unashamedly digress,
I hope that you'll be patient and not think of me the less.

Now in most situations we found we could travel free,
An assault on her would violate what was 'my property'.
So that gentleman of Pakistan had done 'the correct thing',
And when I declined the offer, well he took it on the chin.

The trouble comes when cultures connect uneasily,
With that sexual code imported and with no attempt to ease
Its workings in the western world where other codes hold sway,
Freer and more liberal where love can find its way.

I'm thinking here of what we've seen in cities and in towns,
And how this must be the mindset, that drives the grooming gangs:
Where no man is in the picture there need be no control,
As was seen so very clearly some years back in Cologne.

And sadly too, the women can be quite aligned with this,
Their boys 'are blameless, it's the West, the girls just ask for it';
Someone told of desperate mothers hoping that they'd intercede,
The Pakistani Centre's door was slammed – no trace of 'ruth or rede'.

But a shameful racist legacy means we can't see this plain.
So, from fear of being in its wake, the Law itself abstained.
Forgotten was the motto – 'The Children of the Poor Defend',
A craven outlook took its place – 'Watch Out We Don't Offend'.

And this was then the vacuum that the grooming gangs enjoyed:
To act out with impunity and work their countless ploys,
To prey on the weak and vulnerable who needed care and love,
They gamed with them unhindered by officials credulous.

Now UK judges often say 'You treated her like meat,
Did you have no feeling for her?' Where was your empathy?'
But to a member of a grooming gang, no laws had they disturbed,
For the young girls that they preyed on were of so little worth.

And defending lawyers argue then to plead the case away,
'M'Lord my client's culture was what led him astray',
Which just bears out our Shappi's joke about her native land:
'You think Britain has hang-ups – well you should see Iran!'

I write not to stir up anger, but try to analyse,
These awful crimes which perpetrators think are authorised;
And stand up for the value of the poet's fine ideal:
'Man and woman equal, loving, confident and free'.

These Baklava On My Plate
(I Sing of Bad Theology)

These baklava on my plate,
Are like those used to celebrate,
The holding of a pogrom new:
We all heard of people who,
Handed out the little treat,
To rejoicers in the street.

I wonder what theology,
Could lead to this unholy glee?
I wonder just what worthless dross,
Could such hate have put across?

I say I wonder, actually,
There is no hidden mystery,
About the hate too often taught,
That influences childhood thought.

Described by one, an unspoiled girl,
But with a teacher who unfurled,
A burning hatred of the Jews,
Which in later life she overthrew.

Sister Aziza was that teacher,
There to guide the youngsters' minds,
But with a doctrine full of hate,
She sought accord to undermine.

So she taught to curse the Jews,
The worst insult that could be used,
And pray for their annihilation,
Or their total subjugation.

Sister Aziza told the children
How the Jews had horns and tails,
Not only monstrous in appearance
But destined sure to burn in hell.

It sickens me to cite these libels,
But they're something to be faced,
Not just brushed under the carpet,
Out of some respect misplaced.

So when a killer, on that day,
Proudly phoned his Mum to say:
'Ma, I've just killed full ten Jews —
Tell the family the news!'

His murders must have been related
To these doctrines inculcated.
Had they been challenged in his mosque?
Or how had they been put across?

He thought he drew on scholarship,
And what was said in Holy Writ;
His acts must have been incubated
With no opposition stated.

And sadly, in Muhammad's book,
There's a strain that has this look;
Most often by believers faced,
And with a tolerance replaced.

But as of now, as I write here,
UK police have witness clear,
Of three imams who've counselled hate,
To divide and separate:

'Curse the Jews and unbelievers,
Shake the ground beneath their feet;
Kill the unrighteous where you meet them,
Destroy their homes, their ranks deplete.

'Scatter them and make them slaves,
Make them captives of the pure,
Freeze the blood inside their veins,
Curse them all for evermore'.

Again, I hate to cite these libels,
Again, they're something to be faced;
Again, not brushed under the carpet
Out of some respect misplaced.

They came from listed charities,
These charmless calls for genocide,
The Charity Commission then weighed in,
Ruled against one … who later sighed:

'No, no, I have done nothing wrong,
Those are the words from scripture's book;
They're just about the end of days,
I invite you all to go and look.

'They come direct from Allah's messenger,
And deep in the Hadith they lie'.
The Commission though was not impressed,
And ruled he was disqualified:

'For he had stoked division, hatred,
And by the group it must be noted,
We're warning them to take great care,
When such violent words are quoted'.

And that bears out what I said earlier,
On watching when the book holds sway;
And drawing lines at that 'bad doctrine
Which can lead the vulnerable astray'.

At least he had been made aware,
There was a wider world out there,
And our culture democratic,
Had touched upon his mindset static.

But also think – I'd say you must not
Thinking Muslims, here discount;
I'll bet they had a role in helping
Bring him and the others to account.

They don't want such rabble-rousers,
They make their lives a misery,
Just leading up a human dead-end,
Paved with stones of bigotry.

So, next time, if a baklava,
Is there sitting on my plate,
And memories of gleeful hatred
To my thoughts should penetrate,

I will not let them overwhelm,
Or lead to desolation's brink,
But, upon such thinking Muslims,
I will try to also think.

A Poem for Gaza's Young

The children came from the West Bank,
And were taken to a country field,
In the Oxfordshire surroundings,
Where they, amazed, could Freedom feel.

They could just run into the distance,
Let their faces feel the air,
No milieu of war around them,
No hidden mines they must beware.

There are two sides to every story,
And this one has a bitter past,
Each side with its inner logic,
A history that is built to last.

One can argue to and fro,
Both sides of this long-lasting strife,
But that will yield precisely nothing
In terms of one young person's life.

They dream of being doctors, teachers,
Computer whizzkids, engineers,
Their potential unrestricted,
But cast away by ancient fears.

The way of violence reinforces
Those sad patterns of the past,
Non-violence the way for both sides
At least to co-exist at last.

So those kids can have a future,
Not bound up with forever war,
And their kids can walk the fields,
Take fearless steps as once before.

A Praise Song

Gracious, courteous, kind, hardworking,
Since Medina came to town,
Our lives have had a clear improvement,
We talk of all the things we've found:

Watermelons, plums, papayas,
Oranges, tomatoes too,
Glistening in cardboard boxes
Bulging onion sacks on view.

Spices, teas, exotic coffees,
Fresh herbs to lift the dullest dish,
Pulses, chutneys, dosa mixture,
All the dates that one could wish.

Round the back there's halal meat
I have to say that I avoid,
For reasons of animal welfare –
And yet I stay quite unannoyed.

For my old Mum is in her nineties,
And had a turn outside the shop,
Grabbed a lamppost, went all white,
And to the ground she slowly dropped.

The young man on deliveries
Quickly came and brought a chair,
And as she sat and closed her eyes
The manager we saw was there

Who then whipped out his mobile phone,
And for an ambulance did call;
And stayed there till it had arrived,
And she was in its space installed.

And, since then, we always stop,
And have a smile and little chat:
'How's your Mum a-getting on?'
We talk of this and talk of that.

So let us sing to praise Medina,
A praise song as in days of old;
For they have found the righteous path,
Not burning hot or icy cold.

'Work is Love made visible',
So said Gibran, the Lebanese sage;
And Dr Johnson, our own wise man,
Said much the same in former age.

For he opined that 'Man is seldom
Occupied so innocently,
As when he is making money',
So let us all on that agree.

For a Christian-heritage, secular culture
Has many points at which it strays,
From the views of old Islam
And never will be brought to change.

So it is best to put those disputes
To one side and try to nourish,
Ourselves, as well as those around,
So future generations flourish.

And let us sing to praise Medina,
A praise song as in days of old;
For they have found the righteous path,
Not burning hot or icy cold.

Stanzas on Ukraine

From 1968 to 2022…

It was subjugation, pure and simple, back in '68:
The tanks rolled in, the people stood,
And looked on their unfolding fate.

They told the soldiers on the tanks:
'Go home! We just don't want you here';
But in spite of all their righteous rage,
They could not make them disappear.

So Dubcek's way was overthrown,
The Soviet lesson was enforced;
For a few more years at least,
Before it ran its sorry course.

And fifty years later on,
On subjugation task,
Another line of tanks rolled in,
But were met with rocket blasts.

Citizens and soldiers,
With quad bikes spied, and aimed
The mobile rockets from their friends,
And through the air they flamed.

That long, long, long, long convoy,
Of tanks stopped in the snow,
And as the world watched on in awe,
No further did they go.

Meanwhile, and nearer Kiev itself,
A Ukrainian who knew,
How nearby airports were a key,
As an invasion grew,

For lifting troops in, all their stuff,
To build a presence there,
And overwhelm defences,
Reinforcing from the air,

Gathered up then with his mates,
Lorries, trucks and vans,
And parked them on the airstrip near,
So the aircraft could not land.

They heard the planes approaching,
They circled, not quite sure,
And then flew off frustrated,
And so were seen no more.

They know what subjugation means,
And against it they will fight;
Even as the dark descends,
And they face the Russian might...

What Gives You the Right?

Russia, O Russia,
Do we see you now plain,
With your masses complicit in crime?
Though your brave marchers few,
Quickly hustled from view,
May redeem in the passage of time.

What gives you the right,
With such malice and spite,
To lay others' cities to waste?
Because of one man,
And his barbarous plan,
Is your land not forever disgraced?

And don't you recall,
How back in the war,
Your people were bombed and displaced?
And how you take pride,
In how they defied,
The Nazis and to them laid waste?

Now don't you defile,
Through this warfare so vile,
Their devotion and blood sacrifice?
And hospital wards,
And refugee hordes,
Reveal its so pitiful price?

A young girl in tears,
For the pets that she'd left,
To starve in the rubble of town;
And flats opened wide,
To the cold air outside,
By brutish bombs raining on down.

The stories of pain,
Which again and again,
Are transmitted over the news;
Are too overwhelming,
To lay out in verse,
But will be long in the memory fused.

Now let the gentle, the free and the brave,
Step up to the challenge laid down,
Now let the lawmakers, crunchers of numbers
Work out the amends to be found.

Now let the fighters and warriors true,
Who here do an Empire resist,
Find that their strivings are met with success,
With peace no more crudely dismissed.

And Russia, O Russia,
May you discover,
The way to the pathways of ruth,
And not harden your heart,
To forever depart,
But open your eyes to the truth.

Law No More

Is there anything else,
That now may attract,
The ire of a spurned President?
Some land that he thinks,
Was wrongly assigned,
With the wrong people there resident?

Some country he feels,
Is too close and too flat,
To repel the attacks that will come?
So should occupied be,
And no longer be free,
So in future those deeds won't be done.

Will his fancy alight,
One day or one night,
On a new project to be fulfilled?
If so you should know,
That his acts won't be slowed,
By the prospect of blood to be spilled.

International law,
Doesn't feature at all,
In the mind of a man so obsessed;
And the great world of all,
Its concerns and its laws,
Are there merely to be suppressed.

So now it is certain,
No veil and no curtain,
A wrong 'un is out on the loose;
With blood on his hands,
Casting ruin on lands,
And all for his dreams of Old Rus.

Machiavelli it's said,
Had tactics so dread,
They would take everyone by surprise;
But taken in once,
(Maybe taken in twice),
Then everyone's used to your lies.

In the end there's a natural
Yearning for justice,
Ingrained in the lives we enjoy;
And that force will arise,
And then mobilise,
In Freedom's cause to be employed.

He's Just a Common Thief

Today's dictator blusters,
Alone and on the stand,
With visions false of destiny,
And claims to Ukraine's land.

The truth is more prosaic,
He's just a common thief,
Who wants his hands on Ukraine's gold,
Its cornfields and its beef.

He knows the Russia he has made,
Is critically bereft,
And having spurned creative paths,
Can see no options left.

So all this stuff 'bout NATO,
And Nazis ruling Kiev,
And Western wrongs that threaten still,
Are smokescreens to deceive.

The truth is more prosaic,
He's just a common thief,
Who wants his hands on Ukraine's gold,
Its cornfields and its beef.

Churchill said that Russia hides,
In mystery, riddle twined,
All wrapped in an enigma,
But here's his final line:

It's Russia's raw self-interest,
That gives the vital clue,
That will be the key he said,
And now as then it's true.

So think of coal and wheat and oil,
And warm sea-water ports,
Those will animate his thoughts and dreams,
Till he's to justice brought.

Ukraine Dreamin'

Come on, let's dream a better future,
Than the current horror show,
As laid out by a writer exiled,
From Putin-land he'd had to go.

Bearded, from a small room talking,
With an uncertain life ahead,
'How should things be?' the question came,
And this is roughly what he said:

'Ukraine and Russia have a past,
Entwined in history's passing flow,
Closely bound and complicated,
But from that past we have to go!

'We have to think of both proud peoples,
And their future lives and wealth,
And how to build prosperity,
And how to build well-being, health,

'For the children of the future,
So they perish not in mud and snow,
Fighting for an old idea,
No, from that past we have to go!

'Catherine the Great and Greater Russia,
Tsarist dreams and Stalin's crimes,
The coveting of wheatfield bounty,
No, we must leave all that behind!

'I can see a path ahead,
Where our lands can safely go,
And our descendants forward tread,
Into the future they can grow.

'As a Russian I pay tribute,
To the skills and industries,
Of Ukraine and its fine people –
If they can thrive then why can't we?

'If Ukraine wants to face the West,
Well, that's the way they want to go;
And so the path of least resistance,
Is found by going with the flow.

'In the world we now inhabit,
We should be partners for the greater good:
Ukraine draws on Russian resources,
Russia deals in trade not blood.

'It would gain by resource trading,
Its people gain from profit shared;
Ukraine busied with its business,
And the world from hunger spared.

'So that's it, it's so damn simple,
So damn simple – one, two, three!
So let's cast off that bad old thinking,
And as partners, neighbours be'.

And with that the image flickered,
And with that he disappeared,
Leaving me to mourn the now,
Yet with a sense of foresight clear.

...and on to 2025

...and now it's full three years in,
With a heavy price now paid:
In captured land, in children thieved,
In the lines of soldiers' graves.

But they know subjugation,
And won't have it no more:
It's progress on from '68,
That submission is no more.

A BYRONIC FABLE:
in which Lord Byron and Joe Biden reflect on Afghanistan and Greece

Enter ... Joe Biden

To think that we spent twenty years,
To lead this backward land from tears!
Blood and treasure in the sand,
Lost for this unyielding land!

I opposed it from the start,
You cannot change these people's hearts;
And for some girls in Kabul's needs,
I will not let my soldiers bleed.

And please don't talk of poetry,
That world is simple, trouble-free,
And name me just one poet who,
Has once for Freedom given his due.

Go on, name one, here I am:
US President, Joe Biden!
Come on, you conjure from the shades,
Just one who has a difference made!

THERE IS A CRACK 0F THUNDER, LIGHTS FLICKER
AND THEN THERE IS HEARD THE TAPPING OF A STICK.....

Enter ... Lord Byron

Well I was resting when I heard,
From somewhere else a far-off word,
Summoning me with living breath,
From my rest in peaceful death.

Ah, I see, a President,
Of the USA has some intent,
To hear of my last voyage to Greece,
So that an Empire's grasp would cease.

From a Yankee, I would say,
I would rather, any day,
Have a little nod, a signal small,
Than an Emperor's gift bejewelled.

He scorns the poets – I agree!
No dissent he'll have from me.
A scribbler's life is not complete,
They must in the world compete.

So of that voyage to Greece I'll tell,
And draw out every parallel,
Along the way so you can see,
How runs the highway of the free.

So, Joe, let me please interject,
And show where centuries intersect;
For the purpose of this play,
I can here all things survey.

Now both Greece and Afghanistan,
Shared their warlords, tribes and clans;
Both with local rivalries,
That had festered on for centuries.

And there the balances of power,
Are watched like hawks from hour to hour.
Allegiances will change in length,
According to perceivéd strength.

So when news came, that I had made,
A loan, for ships towards Greece to sail,
Othman's navy would withdraw,
From posts by Missolonghi's shore.

And when news of my death was heard,
Supplies and credit were deferred;
Volunteers faltered in their tallies,
Because round me they could not rally.

Thus when support from Afghans brave,
Who fought their country for to save,
Was cut, to leave them there forlorn,
A fatal signal sounded forth.

Now you've complained of money's waste
By those corrupt – a true disgrace!
And why should Uncle Sam, you say,
For those corrupt and disloyal pay?

Those Afghans loyal to tricks were put:
So some could claim a bigger cut.
Their officers would the listings swell,
Neglecting them, their needs as well.

It was just the same for me:
I made the sad discovery,
That officers of my fine Brigade,
Had claimed and creamed off phantom pay.

Captains, majors conjured up,
So that they could better sup,
Tribesmen promoted beyond their dreams,
I raged when I unearthed their schemes.

In the end I closed that down,
With the chieftains had a mighty row,
Though I understood, it showed,
I had to league with charming rogues.

They were like our Highlanders of old:
Ungovernable, but brave and bold;
And in the end they had loved me,
The parting songs true eulogies.

I'll also add, Joe Biden, here;
A crucial thing must now appear:
A strategic point that came to fore,
Some years after I was no more.

Greece, part of Empire Ottoman,
Whose ships made sure their writ would run;
When Navarino cut that link,
Then for sure their star would sink.

Those they call the Taliban,
Found haven sure in Pakistan.
So I'd say if you'd cut that link
Their fortunes would have had to sink.

In the end the reasons you
Had found that, that, you could not do,
Meant in the end you could not win,
But your example may yet spin

A future different in that land –
Can anyone those barbarians stand?
When they've had a glimpse of light,
Good government at least in sight.

The Greeks, the Greeks, to me they'd say,
Could not be trusted night or day,
But to them I would reply:
'Redeeming qualities you will find

In the humble countryman,
Corrupted not by devious plan;
And when at last misrule will lift
You'll find, maybe, that things will shift'.

One final thing I'll say to you:
Towards the land of Greece I threw,
My energies, alert to those,
Warlords brave whose actions showed

Their visions were but localised,
To rule the roost with their own tribe.
My words, my acts, a demonstration,
Not for a faction but a nation.

That country soon would come to be,
Independent, proud and free:
The first true nation European,
For her – deserved poetic paean!

Joe Biden:

Well, Lord Byron, it has been,
A privilege to meet you here;
And I must withdraw my hasty words,
That poets all are quite absurd.

For you made a sacrifice,
Your fame, your fortune and your life;
I abandoned Freedom's cause,
And took the politician's course.

Realpolitik, my dear Lord B,
Scorned by you, vital for me;
You lost your life in foreign land,
But by my judgement I must stand.

That blood was never mine to shed,
That treasure earned by those instead,
Who cared not of these foreign lands,
– So by my ruling I must stand.

Sure, me and Kamala regret,
The lives that now seem all too set,
On women, forced by Taliban men,
Returned to homes and robbed of pen

And of potential – chattels and,
Their contributions to their land,
Wished away and cruel ignored,
With faces to be seen no more.

But me and Kamala sleep at night,
Oh yes we do, for might is right.
There is what is, and what might be,
But that is not for us to see.

A BEATLES FABLE:
in which Hitler
has a nightmare
of a Yellow Submarine

Bombs fall down on Liverpool, baby Beatles in their beds,
The docks it's said the target was; but did they aim for them instead?
For though war's vital sinews fill the military mind,
Might we in Hitler's addled brain a darker motive find?

Imagine him with Goering, one 1940s morn,
Looking from his desk at him, with sunken features drawn;
With Goering so surprised that day to see him in this state,
In those times of triumph he was normally elate.

'Mein Führer … are you quite alright?' he hesitantly began —
Hitler simply silenced him, with a wave of his right hand;
'Hermann, oh my Hermann', he whispered soft and low,
'Last night I had a dream that could a wretched future show.

'Even now that dream's within, and hanging over me,
Bringing what I never feel … a vile uncertainty;
I feel sick and listless, my confidence has gone,
I see shadows of catastrophe that stretch so far and long'.

'Mein Führer', replied Goering, 'May I loyally protest?
A dream is just a nothing and within a nothing dressed;
Mein Führer, please remember, it is as they say:
You are literally the master of all that you survey'.

'The Poles are routed, France has fallen, Russia's bear quakes too,
That Churchill is a gangster drunk who'll shortly kneel to you;
Your armies are the finest, your Panzer tanks unmatched,
No Spitfire can the fighter planes of our Luftwaffe catch.

'Forgive me, please, mein Führer, but may I be so bold
To ask you why you speak of dreams when opened is the road
To the Reich which will last glorious, a thousand years and more,
And your name and great achievements will live on for evermore'.

'Hermann, oh my Hermann, by your loyalty I am touched,
But History is bound to say: you were no great genius!
If this dream should come to pass, our goals will be forestalled,
And our Thousand-Year Reich, just picture it, will fall'.

'May I sit, mein Führer?', Goering then replied,
'I must hear this dreadful dream and look it in the eye';
Hitler looked with bloodshot eyes and waved him to a chair,
And then to tell his story he mentally prepared.

'Hermann, oh my Hermann, this was the tenor of my dream,
Which in the darkness of the night did so convincing seem;
I dreamed I saw a country much like tales of Olde England,
All colourful, *ein musikgruppe* there on a bandstand.

'And next there came a character, quite clearly based on me,
Called I think a 'Meanie Blue', and when this he did see,
He then unleashed his forces, and as they outward probed,
That *musikgruppe* was imprisoned in a magic globe.

'Those forces were magnificent, an army all so blue,
With Flying Glove and Snapping Turks and Max the Henchman too,
And over that licentious land they spread and conquered there,
Much as I have done, to all my enemies' despair.

'In fact, the first part of the dream was really quite a treat,
He drained the land of colour and froze people on their feet,
Turned them into statues still with Bonking Apple Men,
And music all was stifled, and the birds fell silent then'.

'That must be much like Poland, for now from what I hear,
Everything is quiet, there's an atmosphere of fear,
Nothing in the shops as well, and all colour too has gone…'
But Goering's interjection had been firmly frowned upon.

'Hermann, oh my Hermann, please don't interrupt my tale,
I'll forget some little something, you'll my train of thought derail;
So I will quickly carry on to the dream's unsettling end,
Then I'll accept your guidance as a colleague and a friend'.

Hitler paused, and then looked up, with bloodshot rheumy eyes,
Again Goering was a little shocked and taken by surprise,
And calling him a friend indeed! he *must* be out of sorts;
Then Hitler recommenced his tale and Goering stilled his thoughts.

'Sadly Hermann, one escaped, the Apple Men had failed,
And in a Yellow Submarine he then set off to sail;
To get to *somewhere*, he was thinking anywhere would do,
And on a morning grey and damp he came to Liverpool.

'A young man he met, called Ringo, who had a group of friends,
One of whom was quite sarcastic, on that you could depend,
One witty and so musical, another one dreamy,
And Ringo was kind-hearted, that you could clearly see.

'Anyway, they there and then, and each in turn agreed,
That they would surely come with him and help him in his need;
And after some adventures, in the seas their journey spanned,
In their Yellow Submarine they reached the conquered land.

'Then when they played their music, in that land so governed well,
The flowers got their colour back, gone was the statues' spell;
The army of the Meanie Blue was turned and put to flight –
Eva said she heard me moaning in the darkness of the night.

'And this was now the really truly terrifying thing:
The sarcastic one came to the fore and then began to sing;
The Snapping Turks, the Dogs of War, even the Flying Glove,
Were vanquished by a song he sang – 'All You Need is Love'.

'All You Need is Love!' said Goering, 'That's awful, and what's more,
Mein Gott! Right now in Liverpool the babies have been born,
Whose destiny is surely to take part in this bad dream,
And in a different future to the one we so esteem'.

'Indeed', answered the Führer, 'the Reich will have been stopped,
If this future happens where the Meanie Blue is mocked;
From nowhere did this vision come and settle strange on me,
And Hermann, oh my Hermann, this is why I fear this dream'.

Goering stood up carefully and dusted off his sleeves,
'Why, mein Führer, I know for sure what would your fears relieve;
I'll kill those babies in their beds, a major raid is planned,
Next week I think, on Liverpool, that nothing can withstand'.

'Good' said Hitler quietly, and the dream began to lift,
And next thing off went Goering, extra pilots to enlist;
But neither thought of Herod, and how his scheming plans,
Had failed to counteract the life of a transforming man.

Forward Thinking

The Rise of Diasporic Lives

The rise of diasporic lives,
Across the countries of the earth,
Bring partings, absence, separations,
From the homelands of their birth.

Left behind there is a silence,
In the rooms where theretofore,
There were living presences,
Now out of sight but dwelt on more.

The elderly are in the minds of
Those who've left and stay elsewhere,
Now too frail for those long journeys,
Visits back to show they care.

So aviation's now hardwired
For families whose lives are torn,
Telecoms its lesser sidekick,
When daily separation's borne.

It's just too much for comprehension,
Children's ties extended are,
Both divides and sudden love-bombs,
Visitations from afar.

Young ones' study, young ones' spirit,
In their new environment,
Which is theirs to live and dream in,
On their forward path now bent.

Daily struggles to establish
Lives in foreign hinterlands,
Some you know breeze through and prosper,
Through skills acquired, with brain and hands.

Others' drive for better living,
Motives of complexity,
Sandy lands or persecution,
The struggle for security.

Or wanting to join up with boyfriend
In a distant foreign land,
Lives defined by hidden forces,
Hindered, helped by hidden hands.

Cultural sharing, cultural mixing,
Easy sometimes, tensions too,
Those interactions myriad,
In vain to craft an overview.

Women from repressive cultures,
Finding room to live and breathe:
Music, cooking, nano-science,
Skills to master and bequeath.

Once we lived in villages,
And then in cities and in towns,
With the feared unknown afar,
But now all life so near is found.

Humanity is on a journey,
Maybe hard for those of greater days,
But those raised in its caravan,
May know and navigate its ways.

For Those Unborn

For those unborn, as yet unloved,
Direct your labours now and here,
Though they may be out of sight,
In time they will for sure appear.

And then you will be strong for them,
Foundations sure well-built to give,
And in the long-term destiny,
Making space to help them live.

A Maxim: All I Can Do

All I can do,
Is all I can do,
And all I can do is enough;
To sleep well at night,
At the end of the day,
At peace with the world
And its stuff.

NOTES, REFERENCES, PHOTOGRAPHS

For a Godson

'My Dad he had a godson,
Who'd never found his feet…'

For Benjamin

'And the first time he arrived…'

The Major, his brother, and his never lived-with lover

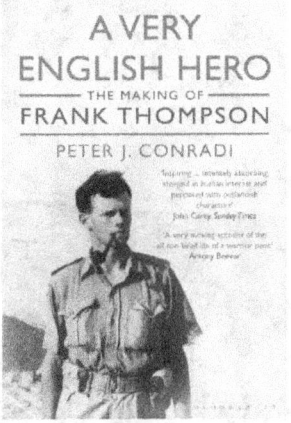

'And Iris Murdoch thought of him, it's guessed,
when she would come to write,
On the persistence of true goodness
when faced with blackest night....'

John Martyn encountered

'And here he was in Nottingham,
and being the main man...'

Mary and the Legacy

'Now these books upon my bookshelf
tell a tale that must be told…'

For Mark

'We walked to the beach together…

… Cliff and bonfire under moon…'

For Jenny and Chris, *en route* to Nice

'And from the Promenade des Anglais
You'll get a marvellous view....'

Stonehaven

'Weathered cliffs and rounded bays, Washed by ever-breaking waves...'

'Hey that was a castle true...'

Byron's Broad Street boyhood

'No trace of Byron's boyhood home, but these surrounds he would have known....'

The Dying Glacier

'With a blue and patient eye
Looks out upon its fate....'

'Thank You, Fog the Second'

'It was like a fog descended
Just like in Auden's day...'

The Weightiest Places

'A spacious old colonial dream…'

'I caught my breath when I espied….'

'At the spot a statue stands:
Allende's image and last words…'

'Another photo showed the bombers
Up on high above the land…'

On Shafilea Ahmed
https://en.wikipedia.org/wiki/Murder_of_Shafilea_Ahmed

These Baklava on my Plate
(I Sing of Bad Theology)
'Sister Aziza taught the children…'
As told by Ayaan Hirsi Ali
https://www.pressreader.com/uk/daily-mail/20231014/281822878459006

'And sadly in Muhammad's book
There's a strain that has this look
Most often by believers faced
And with a tolerance replaced…'

There are nearly 110 verses on the Koran advocating violence against 'infidels'. An example of a modern Muslim approach to them can be found at https://muslimculturehub.com/what-does-the-quran-say-about-infidels/

The Charity Commission's judgements on mosques accused of hate speech can be found at https://www.gov.uk/government/news/places-of-worship-warned-by-regulator-over-inflammatory-and-divisive-language
https://www.brightonandhovenews.org/2025/01/22/failings-found-at-mosque-as-trustee-jailed-for-inciting-jihad/

'No I have done nothing wrong…'

https://www.nottinghampost.com/news/nottingham-news/preacher-who-said-muslims-kill-10328547

A BYRONIC FABLE

Find the story of Byron's Greek intervention here

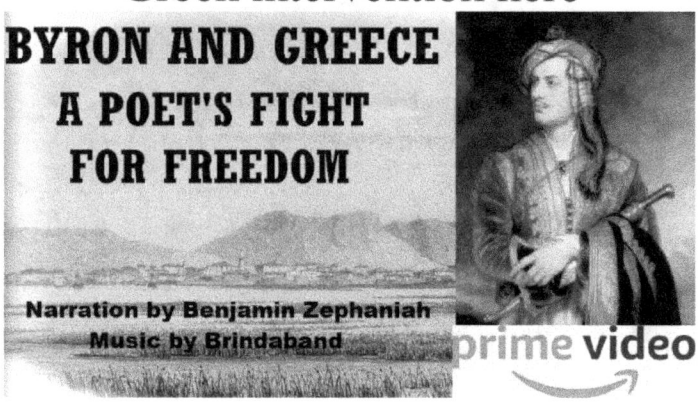

https://www.amazon.co.uk/gp/video/detail/0PDPX9UN9STFBA9KY49M4RLWKB/ref=atv_dp_share_mv

A BEATLES FABLE

'Bombs fall down on Liverpool…'

ALSO BY JOHN WEBSTER

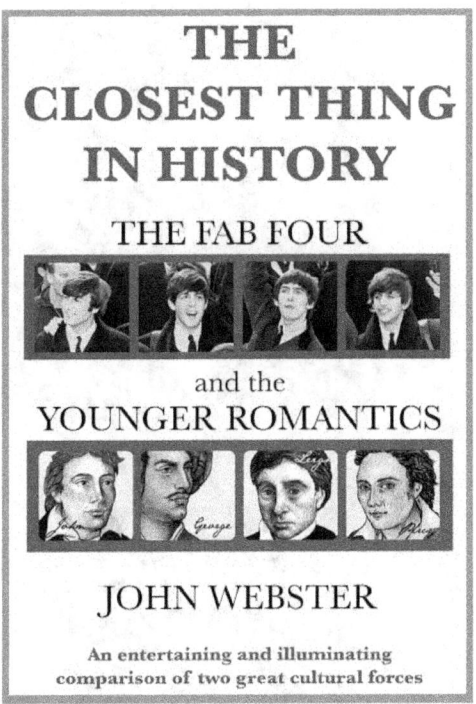

'A CLEVER AND FASCINATING ANGLE ON THE BEATLES'

'The premise that links these fiery, inspired and frankly shocking poets with The Beatles is beautifully argued … Absolutely fascinating.' Boff Whalley, RnR magazine

'MORE THAN A WORDSWORTH OF PRAISE FOR THIS NEW BOOK'

'This wonderful book … is extremely informative and entertaining. Many of the parallels he draws are quite frankly, astounding' John 'Buzz' Bezzini, beatlesbookstore.com

details at
www.johnmwebster.co.uk

www.ingramcontent.com/pod-product-compliance
Lightning Source LLC
Chambersburg PA
CBHW052100070526
44584CB00017B/2261